Praise for *From the Cow's Eye & Other Poems*

Rocks, trees, a 'scalped barn,' a tree named Gretel, winter's muscles bulging with cold, the starving caterpillar of January—Loretta Diane Walker finds personalities in everything—even cancer, even fear, even love. Like the Guernsey cow in this chapbook's title, Loretta sees what was and what is. The uniqueness of her vision is simply stunning. She leaves me gasping for more.

—Barbara Blanks, former editor of *A Galaxy of Verse*, and author of nine books.

This book would have you believe it is full of nature poems, but from the first poem, we travel the *forked road that lives inside* the poet and while we do see much beauty along the way, it is often barren, stingy, withered, stormy and broken. The landscapes we visit include the poet's own body-scape: *No leaves hang from the limb of your body/Your barrenness is imperfect beauty.* Longing, lack, choice, death, hope and fate are juxtaposed in eloquent metaphors blooming amid stunning imagery: *...four leaves clutching/a bony limb on the naked maple.* Narratives of storms and houses, trees and skies bleed into and become metaphor for the body and the forked road it travels as they, and this poet *refuse to silence the beauty.* This book is brave and full of grit. Read it and heal.

—d. ellis phelps, poet, editor, *what she holds,* Moon Shadow Sanctuary Press, 2020.

"'*From the Cow's Eye'* is set in fields of waving metaphor, in images that will seed themselves into your heart. A master of both attention and invention, Loretta Diane Walker has crafted a geography of her own making grounded in everyday imagery yet willing to 'swerve across safety's solid white line'. This small yet diverse collection takes leaps of subject, place and theme, and its poems invite the reader to encounter surprising layers of grief, joy and beauty in each line and landscape. It is a vivid testament to what is good in the world."

—Lisa Toth Salinas, Poetry Society of Texas Eakin Award Winner, 2014.

I enjoyed serving as judge for this manuscript contest. I was impressed with the writings, subjects, and use of words by all the poets. There were some special qualities I liked about the winning manuscript including the words used in each poem's last line. Also, each poem offered a unique structure and expression of words that urges the reader to read slowly to get their true meanings. From the poem titles and contents of this winning manuscript, one can feel that the author has experienced life from different perspectives and possesses deep emotions that are searching for understanding.

—Manny English, Ph.D.

Loretta Diane Walker is a Texas poetic treasure. Her Barney Award-winning book, *From the Cow's Eye & Other Poems,* demonstrates once again both her wonderful imagination and her poetic insight into the human heart.

—Michael Baldwin, winner of the Eakin Poetry Prize, 2011 and the Morris Chapbook Prize, 2012.

From the Cow's Eye
And Other Poems

Loretta Diane Walker

Winner of the William D. Barney Memorial Chapbook Prize, 2021, from The Fort Worth Poetry Society

Fort Worth Poetry Society| Fort Worth, Texas

Loretta Diane Walker/FWPS Books
Fort Worth, Texas

Publisher's Note: This is a work of fiction. Names, characters, places, and incidents are a product of the author's imagination. Locales and public names are sometimes used for atmospheric purposes. Any resemblance to actual people, living or dead, or to businesses, companies, events, institutions, or locales is completely coincidental.

***From the Cow's Eye & Other Poems*/Loretta Diane Walker**.
-- 1st ed.
Cover image, Gigi, by Heidi Lowell <heidi@heidilowell.art>

ISBN 9798512490013

This book is dedicated to Mark, Kimberly, and Jamarkus Schiff. Thank you all for twice nursing me back to health.

A heartfelt thank you to Dr. Manny English for selecting *From the Cow's Eye and Other Poems* as winner of The William D. Barney Memorial Chapbook Contest, 2021, the Fort Worth Poetry Society, to Heidi Lowell for her cover design, Abby Hullin for the author photo, Barbara Blanks for pointing out "the little things," and of course, my family and friends who have supported my efforts for many years.

TABLE OF CONTENTS

When A Road Lives Inside You, There Are Always Forks

"I am a deer standing away in the dusk ..."
— N. Scott Momaday

1
The mustang canters through a Texas spring.
In a shaggy field, the bold fragrances of lantanas, paintbrushes,
bluebonnets ride bareback, their odors clutch fast the horse's
unruly mane.
2
You are a six-year-old in Sunday school
where summer scrubs the church's dirty white
paint with buckets of sun. You plant flowers
in *The Hanging Gardens of Babylon*
with broken crayons.
3
You are a hungry doe at dusk
in Robert Frost's yellow woods.
Eyes wide with light, back to the wind,
you listen for crows dancing on leaves.
4
You are a Cheshire cat in a tree.
Alice's sly spirit guide. Pretentious, how you
direct her to the mad tea party.
Why is paradise someone else's backyard?
5
Why does that feathery neon arrow
perpetually point to a place of longing?
No matter the direction, you cannot plant
gardenias on the horizon's endless slope.
6
You snuggle in December's fading lap,
slurp chai, wish for summer,
watch a glittery ball drop,
as the air in Times Square burns
with smoky red promise.

7

Curious, how seconds plunge us into the future.
A wisp of breath, the present becomes the past.
Choice is a tattered map
flapping down the universe’s fated side streets.

On the Way to Albuquerque

I head out shadowing dawn's faded crimson face
and the stingy-cheeked clouds drifting in its sky.
Mesquite trees, barren beauty, and the stench
of cow dung and crude crowd the stretch
between Odessa and Roswell.

Buddy Guy's visceral guitar licks,
the tires' incessant rolling,
and this cancer I am trying to convince
a body is not for lease,
spar for my attention.

After one-hundred fifty miles, I rest my vehicle
in a withered grassy patch on the side
of the highway, stretch, shake sleep from my
legs, snap a retired barn's photo.
An intriguing old thing—
metal body streaked with rust.
Scalped roof an altar for air and crows,
unhinged door a hammock for ants and spiders.

After driving five hours, my thoughts leaf
through hunger, a heavy book in my stomach.
I imagine scripts of glazed doughnuts filling its
pages, settle for a fried burrito
from a convenient store. Isn't conflict
the parable of a spirit—
desire, abstinence, dis/ease?

Oh, if my body read like road signs:
Deer Crossing. No Passing Zone.
Men at Work. Fines Will Double.
Caution. Slow. Stop.
My essence would not swerve across
safety's solid white line

and I would not have to lament the penalty
of pain this illness forces on me thrice.

When I am greeted by the sign
Welcome to Albuquerque,
a swarm of afternoon light droops
from the soffit of the Sandia Mountains
and a new passion for the road spins
inside me like titan windmills.

Herb's Banjo

Herbert "Herb" Hall
(March 28, 1907 – March 5, 1996)
was an American jazz clarinetist
and alto saxophonist. He began on banjo
with the Niles Jazz Band 1923–25).
Hall retired with his wife in Boerne, Texas.

The debate—talent or betrayal.
Talent many may conclude.
As for me, I lean in favor of disloyalty.
Circa 1923 to 1925 Herb and I jam
in the Niles Jazz Band.
For two years, I am his "bee's knees."
When he plucks or strums my fretted neck,
I feel the revel in his fingers,
respond joyously in my twangiest brightest voice.

Now this.
Befuddled, I observe a new ritual—
the wetting of a reed.
He is childlike when he puts it in his mouth,
sucks as if it is a lollipop.
The pleasure in his eyes is a warning.

1926 I get the high-hat.
He woos the clarinet and alto sax,
moves to Louisiana to play
with Kid Augustin Victor and Sidney Desvigne.
Jealousy does not creep in— it's a sudden
dissonant chord in my round bottom.

In '29, he drags those two hotsy-totsies
to San Antonio, makes passionate music
with Don Albert til'1950,
then moves about as if on a constant honeymoon
to Philadelphia with Herman Autrey,
New York with Doc Cheatham,

Europe with Sammy Price.
I miss the shine of adoration.
Is there no end to theirs?

1979 I watch him, hair the color of fresh snow,
eyes closed, body sleek as his beloved clarinet.
He chases his fingers up and down the keys,
soulfully blows *Just a Closer Walk with Thee.*
My strings long for those fingers.
They reach for him from the shallow
dusty grave of his memory.

From the Cow's Eye

A Guernsey cow stands
in history's endless prairie,
face framed by a log fence.
A necklace of sunshine loops
her fawn-colored head.

One eye stares into what was
and the other into what is—
a rough red road dividing
rivers of bluebonnets streaming
past bumpy rocks, yawning canyons,
old oak, pecan and mesquite trees.
It zooms in on other strophes of beauty—
white-haired yuccas, carpets of phlox,
sun-streaked daisies, poppies,
firewheels, and flame-colored paintbrushes.

Guernsey's head moves like a sluggish pulley.
Her other bored eye sweeps beyond
wild grass pitching up the steep walls
of a limestone community and hills
ebbing and flowing like gentle waves.

When she stares back through the vista of time,
her eye rests on a creek the shade of morning
and at a vagabond wind wearing the voices
of eight men carving Boerne's name
into the future with the chisels of their dreams.

George Wilkins Kendall Speaks

Not born, but evolved
to become a child of the pen.
I understand how words live on the page,
how they can change a vision,
the euphoria when they carry me
to prosperity's plush banquet.
This is my upbringing, too.
My words force me:
to endure the gruff giant of prison,
learn the shame of lepers,
experience the power of friendship,
and this disgraceful thing—
have my words abducted, compelled
to live in another man's hand,
disguised as his.
Isn't this sin as terrible as war?
Yet I, a humorist, encourage war,
entice it like an insolent foe.
It comes like an invitation,
brings me fame.
After it wounds my knee,
I marry, father four children,
then pen a portrait of its brutal face.
Now a family man, I seek life beyond
the pen, buy twenty-four Spanish
merino rams and a flock of *churro* ewes.
One day I house them
on the Post Oak Springs pasture.
They multiply like the five loaves
of bread and fish as told in a Sunday
school story.
After battling grassfires, blizzards, disease,
I am again, carried to prosperity's plush banquet,
celebrate new fame.
Perhaps out of honor or industry,

kind Texans crown me
“father of the sheep business.”
I wear this title only in death.

Why You Shouldn't Hire the Wind as Your Yardman

1.
Wind will rake dying leaves from mulberry limbs,
smear them on window screens,
drag them across the grassless backyard,
past the naked rose garden,
over the six-foot wooden fence
to the end of your neighbor's white stony alley,
down the six-lane main drag,
and bury them in a gutter
at the intersection of Dixie and 42nd Streets.
2.
If you hire the wind, how can you measure risk?
It's not thrifty with geography,
doesn't care about the difference between Texas
and New York, Chicago and New Mexico,
the boon of a rainbow or the bell curve of COVID.
It will beguile you into believing you
are employed.
But you are a meek lamb seated on a couch,
arms and elbows confined in a wool sweater,
legs and feet bound beneath a fleece blanket.
You will remain there until the evening
stacks stars in the sky, and it stuffs
your memory with the leaves of every tree
you were forbidden to climb as a child.
3.
Wind will listen to Rossini's
William Tell Overture Finale,
match its tempo as it sweeps your carport.
Its presto movement will startle you out
of a dream where you are a mulberry in the middle
of a cotton field.
No one speaks of your beginning
and the past is the only place where your broken
twigs are whole.

No leaves hang from the limb of your body.
Your barrenness is imperfect beauty.

The Fortitude of Leaves

I watch seasons squabble
then make up—
winter's bald mulberries
with spring's budding begonias,
summer's bushy-head oaks
with autumn's straw-colored blades.
Perhaps nature's conflicts
stem from the holding on?
Like these four leaves clutching
a bony limb on the naked maple
in my backyard.
Not a hive of snow nor spurt of wind
can force the ease of their grip.
Such fortitude in the ruff tooth
of these shallow lobes.
How I dismiss grit when this tree flaunts
a glorious green mullet.
When heavy branches hang over a box of light.
When two little girls sit in front of it babbling
because their mouths are full of ice-cream.
How frail these moments—this timeworn giant
outlives one of the little girls.
Thirty-two years since her ascent
above rooftops, the night sky's chamber of stars,
her emptied breaths.
Is death deciduous?
The boundaries of my body
prevent me from climbing
this hulk of maple, my memories—
deeper than its roots.
In the corner of the yard, a lone leaf sleeps
in a bed of white stones as day lazily peels
itself from my window.

West Texas Snow

How beautiful these rare snowflakes,
the way they fall softly against the body,
their touch a small wet manuscript for joy.

All night snowflakes fell.

Between the ellipsis of night and afternoon,
a riotous wind blew.
Now this desert city is moon-colored.
A dense field of flurries clouds the horizon.

I dream this snowstorm is love.
Beneath the throng of flakes, my heart bursts
open from the exuberance of its capricious mood.

Two Years After the Storm

This September morning dismantled the night
with its warm flood of light.
A carcass of moon hangs behind me
as I drive through a neighborhood where houses
are returning to the earth after brutally battered
by hail.
Weeds and grass swarm around the belly of doors,
creep slowly up to the windows' sealed panes.

On a corner lot, neglect sliced gashes
in the roof of a sad white a-frame house—
paint peeling like sunburned skin.
Blackbirds perch on its injured planks,
peek like peeping-toms through slats
down into someone's damaged dream.

And the neighborhood of our bodies?
How will they return to their beginnings—
beyond the night's rank of darkness,
beyond the Milky Way's starry arms,
beyond the beyond,
back to the sea of our mothers' milk?

The cracked arm of a mysterious yard figurine,
juts from behind a squalor of bushes.
I don't care what it is, really.
Maybe some mysteries should remain.
Maybe I should be as that chorus of dandelions,
at the edge of the sidewalk.
No matter how bleak their surroundings,
they refuse to silence the beauty
of their gritty golden melody.

Winter's Gift

I have a new obsession with nakedness.
It started with the tree I named Gretel,
the fruitless mulberry in my backyard.
Now that the heavy green curtains
of leaves are stripped
away, I can see straight through her
long narrow windows of limbs.
The sky has collapsed on Gretel's
wide misshaped head.
Blue, buttery-yellow, and strips of pink
smash against each other, fall beneath
her scaly trunk.
This is the beauty of starkness, to see
the Crayola-colored horizon at a different angle.
Isn't it curious the way a tilt
of head changes vision?

Winter's muscles are bulky, bulge with cold.
Yet Hansel, the pinyon pine in my front yard,
holds fast to his needles, hoards them
like a miser.
Who names trees as if they are pets?
One who is kidnapped, lost
in the deep forest of grief.
Death does this—takes lives,
leaves the living wandering.
Isn't winter a sort of death, too?
The transitional season of mourning?

Last night the west Texas wind screamed
like a banshee, stuffed its mouth
with all sorts of debris—
crumbled gift-wrapping paper,
a plastic chew toy,
a flimsy dollar store welcome mat

to fill its emptiness.
When morning arrives quiet and nude,
I walk ceremoniously bagging
what the wind stockpiled in my yard.
Curious how wispy sorrow feels when carried
Beneath the bright torch of sun, how ripples
of kind words are like breadcrumbs
scattered on the path to joy.

Green Doubled

For Jax

We're both green, that personality
which questions the world,
fact check the ones we trust
out of a desire to know what's beyond...
We take a selfie on a deserted street in Abilene,
two parishioners in a cathedral of silence,
distrust the emptiness,
believe there's more than our quiet breaths.

January

Is a caterpillar,
slowly starving,
a pupa cocooned in silky promises,
a wingless creature
craving flight.

Isn't this the transfiguration,
unfurling tale of a New Year?

To consign our yesterdays
to cinders and dust,
to become a servant of hope,
unseal faith from its belly?

This is the Sketch of a Hallelujah

How glorious this February night.
The sky's dark hand unveils a lambent full moon.
Eager stars giddily flicker with jovial light.
Alas, morning will come too soon.

The sky's dark hand unveils a lambent full moon.
Its round clown-white face beams with delight;
an elm's bare branches are lifted in admiration.

Eager stars giddily flicker with jovial light.
Shadows blanket winter dressed fields.
A scarf of wind dusts away yellowed grass.

Alas, morning comes too soon.
Moon and night shadows disappear.
Lazy stars grudgingly extinguish
their jovial light.

Rejecting the Sky

Bright sky, winter sky, goddess sky,
I try to mute your beauty by closing my eyes
and reveling in the music of sleep.
Is this how we grow?
Push back what gives us delight?
Push back from the banquet table
crowded with trays of the ordinary?
Dishonor what has given strength?

Sky of the beginning, bonnet of myself,
you will not be silenced
not on the page,
not in my dreams,
not in darkness where you chip light
into millions, trillions of stars.

It is day now and I am awake in this dream
of healing and river of prayers.
Don't you think time is a beautiful woman,
an exquisite creature of conflict and delight?
In a few hours, she will flower hues of wonder
across the sky: primrose pink,
honeysuckle orange, lantana gold.

I will embrace each color as if they are words
in little sentences of truth.

Night as Artist

Five days I walk in and out of myself
in the city of Santa Fe.
My senses collect memories as if my body
is a canvas bag.
How they brighten when I hear the notes
of the native flute harmonize with the voice
of a delicate wind.
When I smell the aroma of roasted green chilies
and freshly baked blueberry muffins
drift out through the door of a corner bakery.
When I see the bouquets of oriental poppies,
jimson weed, and white camellia
at the O'Keeffe museum.

Tonight, I rest in a hammock of moonlight
and watch as the dark hand of sky
sketches the city with different shadows.
Curious how the skyline highlights the holy:
Loretto's miracles spiral up and down
stairs crafted by a nameless carpenter.
At *Santuario de Nuestra Senora de Guadalupe,*
a statue of the Virgin Mary is seated at the altar
like a greeter to welcome the lost, believers,
and wondering souls.
At *The Oldest Church, San Miguel* glows
like a beacon in an orange crown of light.

Below that church's ancient wooden cross,
a static bell hangs from a tower where night
stills its sketching.

What is the Secret of the Universe?

She uses the artifact of myth to cleanse her hands.
Broils shrimp instead of frying it.
Crumbles faith like graham crackers
to make crust for a key-lime pie.
Shamelessly wears a vest of stars
over her braless breast.
No matter.
Her broad chest is mistaken as a night sky.

How does she separate time from itself?
Use it as a scalpel to cut away old scars?
She doesn't answer,
just names the mending wound's history.
I desire a path back to the beginning
with no desire to rush to the end
whatever form it fashions itself.
Who else but a dreamer would have such a desire?
Who else but the universe can
hold her unborn children's umbilical cords?

After Water Was Separated from Water

Genesis 2:17... "But you must not eat from the tree of the knowledge of good and evil..." Genesis 3:6 "...she took some and ate it...and he ate it."

When the earth had no countries, water
and darkness were one I tell my poem
as I pour tea from a plastic pitcher into a glass
filled with ice. Poem scoots to the edge
of my fingers, amused by my mud-colored
waterfall. I say, From the deep, a Voice said,
Light. It was so. Water constantly churned,
poured into itself. A Voice said, Separate.
It was so. The earth—air, water, darkness, light.
Again, a Voice spoke into the days and the earth
filled with color and all manner
of living things— flora, fauna, beast, man.
I feel Poem slip, fall from the cliff
of melting ice cubes into the tea.
I smile, say, A Voice said to mankind,
this is your gift, the earth and all therein.
Except for this tree, it is my voice.
Then the Voice gave mankind its own voice.
Silence dams my throat when Poem surfaces,
face anguished, tears pouring into themselves.
Forgive me, I say.
Perhaps this was the face of God
when mankind ate the apple, swallowed
His voice.

Vows, Batman, and Rain

I. Vows
I find a picture of us cuddled on the couch.
Smiling, I whisper your name like a prayer,
swear never to say it again.
But the syllables of who you are
slide across my tongue.
Zip. A broken promise—vows aren't rosaries.

II. Batman
In the temple of my delusion, I fall
in love with Batman. How can *you* not be jealous
of a multilingual polymath
who makes Holmes and Watson look like amateurs?
His mind so brilliant Superman gives him props.
His body—an art of stealth movement.

III. Rain
Someone we both know says, "I don't want to talk
about the weather. It's hot and everybody
can feel it." Weather is not a diplomat,
you cannot tame, confirm it to your will.
See how those brooding gray clouds crowd the sky?
Soon this city will feel the pop
and smack of sticky wet heat.
Batman with his endless flow of disposable cash
cannot bribe that dark nimbus mob.
Rain falls within thought.

IV. Vows
We promise each other "always,"
ignore each other's birthdays,
do not send flowers when our mothers die,
forget the smell of mourning on our skin.
Glad vows aren't rosaries.

V. Batman
Oh, to have his escapology skills.
I would free myself from the words you used
to chain my spirit.

VI. Rain
Thunder claps in four/four meter.
Fat drops thump against glass, stone,
the beginning of evening.

VII. Coalesce
I stare out the window without you on my mind,
drink silence like water, unmask the truth.
Batman is not a fit for my heart.
A robin sings, its trills thread through
the fingered-limbs of a mulberry like rosary beads.
Does strength require absolution?

Rain, that shapeshifter, absconds into the ether,
leaves its footprints on the heads
of bowing sunflowers.

Why I Am Jealous of Aquaman

Sleep is a con artist,
convinces us as we fall.
How tainted this belief.
Offer it a bribe when eyelids
stop fluttering with conviction.
See how long you stay awake.
Wage war against it.
Buck your eyes until the skin is taut as wire.
Sleep sieges us— magnate or pauper,
drags us into a place where the only escape
is through the window of dreams.

I dream I walk a tightrope across an evening sky
roaring with orange flames.
I dream I am a mermaid in Atlantis with Aquaman.
Not because of his superhuman strength.
Not because of the arcane power glow in his eyes.

Not because he wields the Trident of Poseidon,
can visit the museums of oceans,
meander through galleries of coral,
view the pillar coral with its hard fingers,
colonies of staghorn coral with their stony antlers,
the black coral's tiny spines.

I, a desert dweller, plunge to the depths of love
when I first behold the Pacific's mammoth mouth,
smell its briny breath, feel its playful spray.
I want its cold beautiful heart to love me back.
Beauty this big is incapable of loving
mere mortals—an embrace can crush bones.
And sleep? That con artist releases me
into the cold of dawn
as the wind plays a naked mulberry like a violin.

Comparing Dreams with Rose

On the Way to 7-Eleven, bumping elbows,
we stroll down a damp sidewalk on Lindy Street,
the day fresher than new beginnings.
A reprieve from Odessa's dusty Aprils.
We step around puddles, crossover
to University Boulevard where I find,
pocket a rain-soaked quarter.

Rose rubs her hands, kicks wet leaves, tells me,
"My dreams are racing boats. Flashes of vermillion
spraying smoke. Maybe I live too fast."
Before I wax interpreter, she stretches her swan
like neck. I tell her,
"Dream creativity is a deep crater.
Each time a soul steps to its edge
a fissure spreads, then a kaleidoscope
of light sprays the air."

Interrupted by a smile scrolling across her face,
I turn to see the 7-Eleven behind us,
its cheerful sign a playful hand waving good-bye.
Maybe the meaning of some dreams
are birds that were never meant to fly.

A Matter of Dreams

Dream Sequence 1

I dream my right breast is a peacock;
its long tail travels to my navel.
A harem of blue and green feathers
is across my belly like loose dollar bills.
I try to collect their beauty,
feel a boil beneath my tender skin—
dream it is rolled silk.

Dream Sequence 2

I prick my pinkie on the thorn
of an orange rose, the puncture, a sleeping potion
dripping in my veins.
I wake in a city of softness, a place
where angels outnumber stars—
the heavens toss petals of light
on the endless thigh of day.

Princess Diana of Themyscira, Aka Wonder Woman

She's a wonder of a woman ravished by beauty—
78 years of age. No wrinkles. No fat. No pressure
for perfection, already more perfect
than a department store mannequin.
Puberty never scarred her face
with blotches, blemishes, blackheads.
I do not buy her T-shirt.
The power of her shield too flimsy
to resuscitate the past of a bruised little girl
who wears a vacancy sign each day
where innocence used to live.
Each day she fights the myth
you're not enough because of your body
docked inside skin that blends with the night.

II
Di's a cougar prowling
through this ceaseless jungle of time.
Emerges on the other side
with no scratches, scars, scabs of aging.
No ripples of cellulite on her butt or thighs.
Years sit heavy on my body.
Each day this receptacle of years
carries cancer relics.
The right breast a full cup smaller than the left,
lashless eyelids and swollen arm are souvenirs
of chemo's crushing embrace.
Is this jealousy irrational?
I squeeze into a pair of tight jeans,
put on black knee-high boots, walk
like the princess my father never told me I am.

The Troll Testifies Before the Brotherhood Of Trolls: A Monologue

My brother trolls,
leave judgement to the assembly of dandelions
gathered in the court of this meadow.
Your accusations of "shaming" this brotherhood
are premature.
My account is not deceit disguised
in the costume of an excuse,
rather a testimony of what happened.
No. I will not start with once upon a time.
But must admit,
perhaps, greed was my nemesis.
Three times my stomach yelled
at me, a kid wanting to be comforted,
or a gambler waiting on the next hand.
There it was, a goat large enough for a meal.
He swayed my decision when he spoke,
I am but a mere snack.
The child in me beseeched, "Take."
The gambler in me begged, "Pass."
I, a puppet to my own greed, waited.
Again, the child within screamed
and like a sudden ache,
I felt hooves pounding above my head.
Then I saw it, a goat large enough for a feast.
The child in me beseeched, "Take."
The gambler in me begged, "Pass."
I, a puppet to my own greed, waited.
Time delivered, like a promise,
the third goat, massive as my appetite,
trotted onto the bridge.
The child in me beseeched, "Please."
The gambler in me sanctioned, "Play."
With all the fanfare my mother told me never
to exude, I made my presence known.

That goat glared at me
as if I were an inconvenience.
Insulted by its lack of respect and my hunger,
I charged.
We tussled, our bodies rumbling like boulders
down a hill.
When I woke, the bridge was splintered,
and the sky was filled with white chameleons—
lions, birds, and goats.

When I Thought Mother Goose was My Mother

This desert city mimicked a jukebox.
The wind shook windows
as if they were maracas.
Lightning licked the coal-colored darkness
with its quick forked tongue.
Thunder pounded the drum of sky
with an unrhythmic
boom ka boom, boom ka boom, boom ka boom.
Nervous as a wet cat, I struggled
in the heavy hands of fear
before fatigue wrestled me to sleep.

The loud night dunked my body,
raging with hormones and tamoxifen,
into a deep pool of sweat.
I dreamt my father dried my brows,
washed my neck with lavender scented soap,
and held my right hand.
Interrupted by the pouty squeal of my alarm clock,
I woke in the strong arms of morning's light.
It cradled me as if I were an only child.

Morning's Traffic

Faith, this stillness is deception
like the name I just gave you.
A mask of last night's violent rain.
The way it burst from the dark dungeon
of storm clouds.

The hard falling sounded like words
broken into syllables.
What story was the darkness trying to tell?
What's with autumn's complaint?
Raindrops pounded a maple's thirsty trunk.
Isn't it curious how often the needy
endures the hardest blows?
Sometimes the story is the breaking.

Now that the storm has ceased screaming
old obscenities, the wind is a small voice
caught in a drying sky.

This morning's sky traffic is quiet.
Caves of ivory clouds mute the desert
sun's lively light.
A house wren surveys the white horizon
from the perch of a low branch.
Her effervescent voice hidden behind fat leaves
makes the spruce sing.

Her song makes me wonder
if our bodies are ventriloquists.
The shrug of shoulders, tilt of head,
turn of back, smirk of a smile,
the swipe of tongue across the lips.
The sudden silence a gesture can make
one fall into the wrong meaning. Like this kiss.

The Monarch of Morning

"... By morning
I had vanished at least a dozen times
into something better."
—Mary Oliver, "Sleeping in the Forest"

Night's dark kingdom crumbles
after Morning, that ancient drama queen,
punctures the sky with sharp blades of light.

Today she wears her jewel-less yellow crown.
Centuries ago she snubbed diamonds,
rubies, sapphires, emeralds.

She throws herself a lavish reception
with a dawn chorus of thrushes and robins
crooning their mating songs
from high branches of trees.
With morning glories, daisies, and poppies
unveiling their soft faces
before the staring eye of sun.
With waterfalls roaring and rumbling
down steep rough mountains, their laughter
drowning in unimpressed rivers.

After she robes herself
in a seamless gown of words,
she sprays the air
with honeysuckle and jasmine,
surrounds the horizon
with a long blue curtain of sky,
then declares herself a poem.

Acknowledgements

With much gratitude to the editors, I would like to acknowledge the listed publications where some of these poems first appeared.

A Book of the Year: The Poetry Society of Texas
Afrofuturism
Conestoga Zen
Encore Prize Poems: National Federation of State Poetry Societies
Gasconade Review #5
Poetry 2021: Pennsylvania Poetry Society, Inc.
Prize Poems: Pennsylvania Poetry Society, Inc.
San Pedro River Review
Texas Ballot Poetry
Texas Poetry Calendar
Through Layered Limestone: a Texas Hill Country Anthology of Place
Waco Wordfest Anthology
Writing Texas 7

About the Author

Loretta Diane Walker, a musician— tenor saxophonist, a daughter navigating a new world, a teacher who still likes her students, a two-time breast cancer survivor, and an artist who has been humbled and inspired by a collection of remarkable people and poets, is a member of the Texas Institute of Letters, Best of the Net Nominee and a nine-time Pushcart Nominee, won the 2016 Phyllis Wheatley Book Award and the 2011 Bluelight Press Book Award). Loretta was named "Statesman in the Arts" by the Heritage Council of Odessa. Her work has appeared in various literary journals, magazines, and anthologies throughout the United States,

Canada, India, Ireland, and the UK. She has published five collections of poetry. Loretta is a member of the Poetry Society of Texas, Pennsylvania Poetry Society, Permian Basin Poetry Society, The National Federation of State Poetry Societies Inc., and Delta Sigma Theta Sorority, Inc. She received a BME from Texas Tech University and earned a MA from The University of Texas of the Permian Basin. She teaches elementary music at Reagan Magnet School, Odessa, Texas.

Naomi Shihab Nye states, "Loretta Diane Walker writes with compassionate wisdom and insight—her poems restore humanity."

Walkerld1@aol.com

www.ingramcontent.com/pod-product-compliance
Ingram Content Group UK Ltd.
Pitfield, Milton Keynes, MK11 3LW, UK
UKHW021925190726
13853UKWH00002B/859